THIS ART ATTACK ANNUAL BELONGS TO:

£7.99

LET'S HAVE AN ART ATTACK!

INTRO FROM NEIL

Thank goodness it's that time again - time for the Art Attack Annual 2006! Bursting with creative and fun things to make and do, from papier maché projects and painting to drawing techniques and quick attacks, there's something for everyone.

Art Attacking is about having fun, using what you can find around the house and creating your own masterpieces. So, turn the page and let's Art Attack.

Neil Buchanan

WHAT'S INSIDE!

PUT YOUR FOOT

1

Draw a sole shape onto some cardboard box card and cut it out. Roll a length of newspaper into a tube and stick it to the heel end of your sole to form the leg.

2

To make the boot, scrunch up balls of newspaper and tape them to the foot shape. The newspaper at the toe needs to be bigger than the rest.

3

Scrunch up more newspaper into a sausage shape and wrap it round the back of the leg to make the heel. Tape it down securely.

4

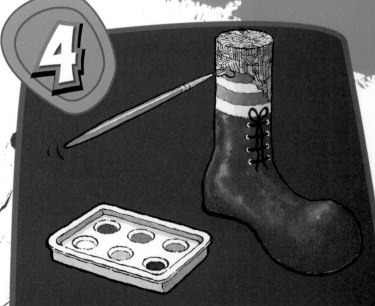

Cover the whole thing with three layers of torn newspaper pasted on with diluted PVA glue. When it's completely dry, paint the boot any colour you like. Draw laces on the front with black marker pen.

YOU WILL NEED:

Cardboard box card, paper, PVA glue, sticky tape, newspaper, kitchen roll, paints, scissors, black marker pen.

5

To make the hole in the ceiling, take a piece of card and draw a dot in the middle. Draw lines from this dot almost to the edge. Make a hole in the centre and cut along all these lines.

6 Roughly tear some white paper triangles and stick them to the card with the points facing inwards. Bend the card and paper outwards so it looks as though it has been burst through. Cut a zig zag shape round the edge.

7 Take another piece of card and paint it black. When it's dry glue it to the back of the other piece.

8 Stick your foot into the hole using glue and sticky tape. Secure it well. Finally stick it to a door or the ceiling.

TO PAINT STRIPES ON THE LEG PART, USE MASKING TAPE TO MARK OFF THE WHITE AREAS. THIS WILL HELP YOU TO GET A STRAIGHT LINE ALL THE WAY AROUND THE LEG!

LET'S DANCE

Use a coloured piece of card as backing.

Create a hair shape and stick that on the card.

Cut out and stick on paler card for the head, neck and arms.

The eyes, nose and mouth are made from black card.

Cut out a dress from red card and glue it in the middle.

Cut out legs and feet and stick them at the bottom of the dress.

Finally create a 3 dimensional flower to fix in her hair.

Make a paper flower for the dancer to hold.

Fold strips of the doily into a concertina shape to make it look frilly.

Cut up a paper doily to make the layered skirt and lace collar.

Add some black shoes with little red circles of paper.

FASHION FUN

BE A FASHION DESIGNER AND CREATE YOUR OWN FUNKY OUTFITS FOR THESE TWO MODELS. USE THE CLOTHES AND ACCESSORIES SUPPLIED AND THEN MAKE UP A FEW OF YOUR OWN.

Trace off and transfer the models onto thick white card.
Then trace the pieces onto the models and colour them
in to create the look you want.

Create other looks by tracing off more models.
What about making your own changes to their hair?

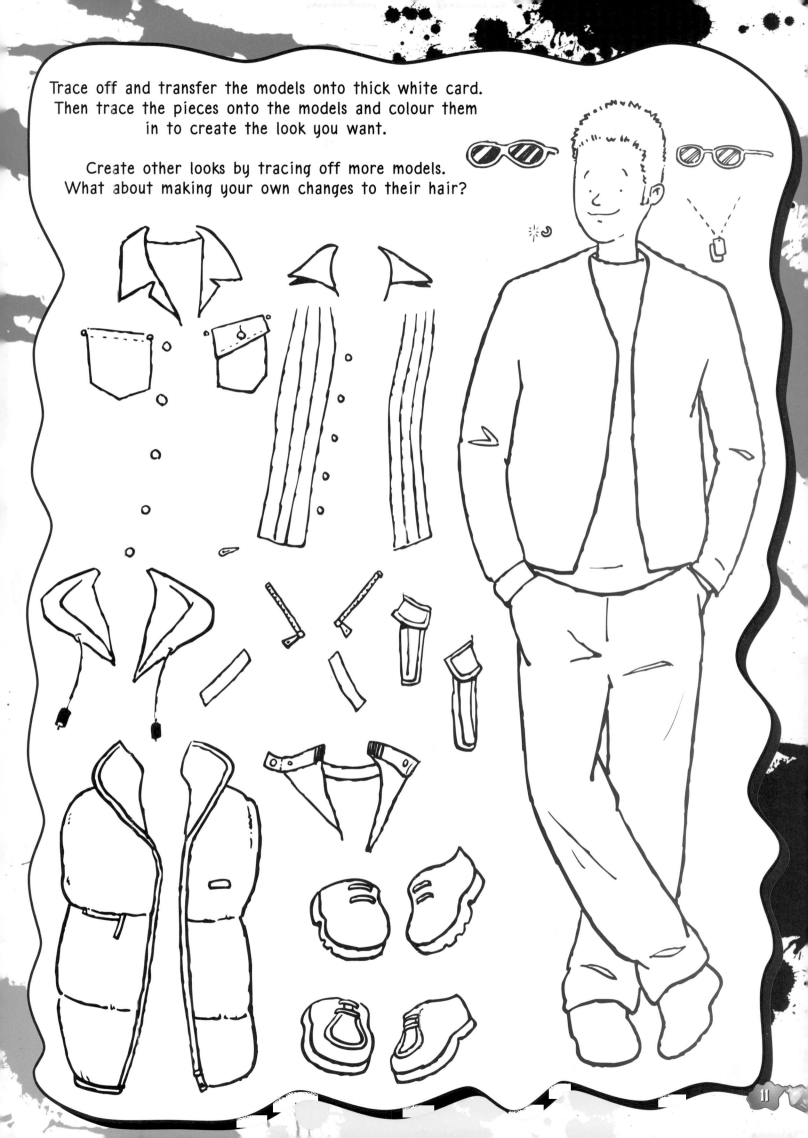

CAT RACK

LETTERS, CARDS AND NOTES ALL OVER THE PLACE? WELL WHAT YOU NEED IS A CUTE CAT RACK TO GET YOURSELF SORTED.

1 Cut a rectanglular base from a cardboard box. Cut out shapes for the cat's head, middle and tail and stick them in place on the base piece.

2 Cut out small rectangles of card and stick them in between each piece to make it stronger. To make the cat's face, stick on a few scraps of card to build up the nose and mouth.

3 Cover the model with about three layers of torn newspaper pasted on with diluted PVA glue, paying attention to the joins. Leave it to dry.

4

Finally paint it. For a ginger cat paint the whole thing white and then orange, leaving some white stripes showing. When it's dry, paint the face and add detail with black marker pen.

YOU WILL NEED:
Cardboard, scissors, sticky tape, newspaper, PVA glue, paints, black marker pen.

TRACE IT

Create a picture that's out of this world by tracing the images below on to the right-hand page. Colour and complete your super space scene!

FLUTTERING FLAGS

MAKE YOUR OWN FLAG THAT ALWAYS LOOKS LIKE IT'S BLOWING IN THE WIND!

1 Cut a flag shape from some cereal box card following this picture as a guide. Roll it loosely.

2 Brush diluted PVA glue over both sides and cover with a layer of torn newspaper strips. Place it between two full or weighted plastic bottles to dry.

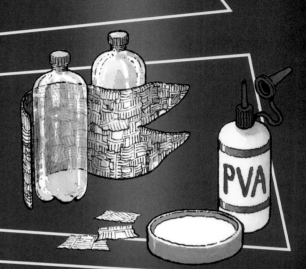

3 When it's dry, tape a stick to the straight edge and add a ball of kitchen paper pulp to the top. Cover it all with papier maché and let it dry.

FINALLY, DECORATE IT! PAINT IN BRIGHT COLOURS OR HAVE A GO AT THIS PIRATE FLAG!

CUCKOO CLOCK

MAKE TIME FOR THIS COOL CLOCK, YOU'LL GO CUCKOO FOR IT!

8 PART ATTACK

YOU WILL NEED:

Cardboard, sticky tape, newspaper, PVA glue, paints, black marker and paper fastener.

17

1 Cut out two pieces of card to make the front and back of your cuckoo clock, copying the shapes above. Cut a rectangular window in one of the pieces.

2 Cut out two rectangular side pieces and tape all the sides together like this.

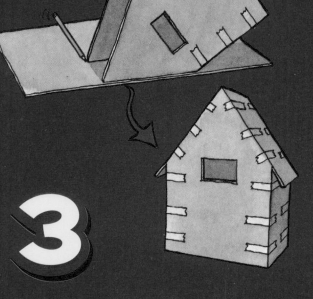

3 Place the clock upside down on some card so you can draw around the roof area and cut out two more pieces of card making them a little longer than the roof as shown. Tape these to the roof.

4 Stick two small doors on the window and then cover the whole structure with three layers of papier maché. Leave it to dry.

5 Draw a small bird shape onto card and cut it out. Cut a slit in the bottom and then paint.

6 Paint the clock. Use permanent black marker to write numbers on the clock face and then make a hole in the middle of it as shown.

7 Cut two clock hands from black card and cut a pendulum from card and paint.

8 Attach the hands to the front of the clock using a paper fastener. Attach the pendulum to the back of the clock face before opening the paper fastener. Finally slot the cuckoo onto the window.

HOW TO DR

IF TRYING TO DRAW PUPPIES SENDS YOU BARKING MAD, LOOK NO FURTHER. HERE IS A SIMPLE GUIDE ON GETTING TO GRIPS WITH THOSE CUTE CANINES!

Draw a round head and peanut shaped body. Add short, chunky legs, a snout, ears and a tail. Then colour.

Try drawing a puppy sitting down. Again, start with a simple oval shape, add some shoulders and mark out where the feet will go. Draw a dotted line in a rough diamond shape to help you position the paws.

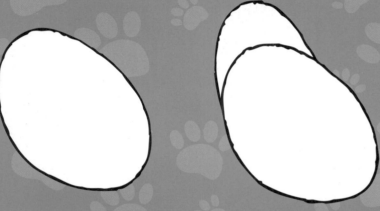

Draw a round head and fill out the outline of the legs. Draw a snout and triangular ear shape. Add details on the face and rub out any unwanted pencil lines. Then colour.

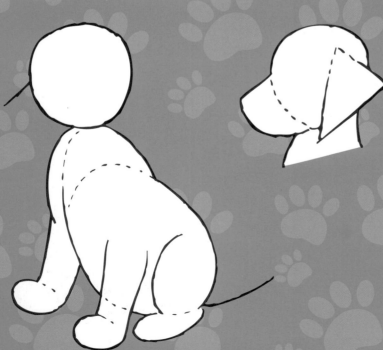

Follow these simple steps to draw this dalmatian puppy. Build up the shapes, improve the outlines and add details before finally colouring and drawing a toy. See how little lines near the tail make him look as though he's wagging it.

Have a go at drawing a running puppy. Take a close look at the position of all the legs to get it right. As he's running the tail and ears will be bent back too.

21

TRY IT YOURSELF

DRAW SOME ADORABLE PUPPIES BELOW USING THE TIPS YOU HAVE LEARNED!

A LOTTA BOTTLE

RECYCLE EMPTY PLASTIC BOTTLES INTO USEFUL STORAGE CONTAINERS.

YOU WILL NEED:
Plastic bottles, scissors, glue, felt tip pens, ribbon or string.

Jelly Beans

Drawing Pins

Sequins

Paper Clips

BEADS

1 Collect empty plastic bottles and clean them well.

2 Draw and colour in all sorts of labels.

3 Cut the labels out and make holes in the top corners.

4 Thread ribbon through the holes and tie in place.

5 Place them round the necks of the bottles.

ART ATTACK

23

GARDEN BOX

GARDENING CAN BE GREAT FUN. MAKE YOUR OWN GARDEN BOX FOR WHEN YOU WANT TO HELP OUT.

1 Make card dividers to go inside a box, a shoe box is ideal. Use sticky tape to secure them inside.

2 Cut out three carrot shapes, two onion shapes and some potato shapes and tape them onto the box. Cut out a card sign and stick it to the back of the box.

3 Build the vegetable shapes up with kitchen roll soaked in a diluted PVA glue mixture and leave it to dry.

4 Stick three straws to the back. Add three flower cut outs to the straws, building up the centre with a ball of pulp.

5 PART ATTACK

YOU WILL NEED:

Cardboard shoe box, card, sticky tape, kitchen roll, newspaper, PVA glue, straws, paint.

GARDEN THINGS

5

Cover the whole thing with three layers of papier maché and leave it to dry. Then paint. Finally write or paint the sign.

ARTY ACTIVI

COPY CAT

Copy the lion into the grid on the right and see how good you are at drroaring!

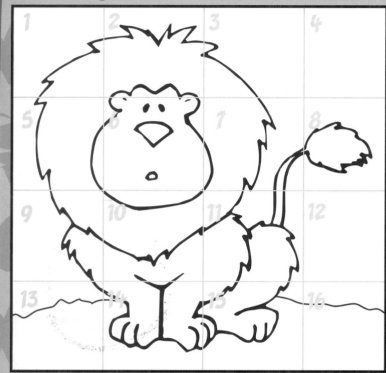

Real Neil?

Look at the images of Neil below and see if you can spot the 5 differences.

1

2

IES

All you need for these mini mind bogglers is a pencil and a sharp eye

GOING POTTY

Look carefully at the 6 paint pots below – can you spot which two are identical?

WORD ATTACK

SEE HOW LONG IT TAKES YOU TO FIND ALL THE WORDS BELOW IN THE GRID!

PAINTBRUSH   SCISSORS
APRON   RUBBER
PENCIL   CRAYON
RULER   PAPER
CHALK   WATER
GLUE   CARD
SPONGE   PVA

A	N	T	U	R	G	E	R	T	C
R	P	A	I	N	T	B	R	U	S	H
R	E	P	K	R	D	E	L	C	A
O	S	N	W	Z	V	P	E	R	L
N	R	D	C	E	X	A	R	A	K
B	O	U	K	I	R	P	S	Y	Z
N	S	P	B	G	L	U	E	O	R
E	S	T	X	B	J	G	D	N	E
R	I	N	W	N	E	I	L	E	T
A	C	A	R	D	O	R	K	J	A
K	S	P	O	N	G	E	A	T	W

27

HOUSE DOCTOR

GIVE THIS SIMPLE HOUSE A QUICK MAKEOVER - YOU CAN MAKE IT INTO YOUR DREAM HOUSE OR MAKE IT LOOK RUN DOWN!

1 Trace the house onto plain card or paper or photocopy it several times.

2 Draw any details that you wish to add such as a TV aerial, satellite dish, letter box, brickwork, ivy, door number, curtains, cat, anything you want.

3 Finally colour everything in using felt tip pens. Add cut outs of window boxes, or planks of wood across the windows depending on the type of house you are creating.

USE YOUR IMAGINATION TO CREATE LOTS OF DIFFERENT TYPES OF HOUSES FROM REALLY OLD TO VERY MODERN.

28

Wobbly Clown

HAVE A LAUGH MAKING THIS CRACKING CLOWN! HE WIBBLES, HE WOBBLES BUT HE WON'T FALL DOWN...

5 PART ATTACK

1 Cover two blown up balloons with four layers of torn newspaper pasted on with diluted PVA glue, don't paper over the knot. One should be larger than the other. Use a bowl to support them as they dry.

PVA

2 Pop the balloons and remove the pieces. Secure a large piece of sticky tack or modelling clay to the bottom of the larger balloon.

3 Join the head and the body together with sticky tape and then cover the whole thing with another two layers of papier maché. Leave it to dry.

PVA

30

2 balloons, newspaper, PVA glue, bowl, sticky tape, clay or sticky tack, paint, wool, paper, pom poms or old buttons.

4 When it's dry, paint it white. When that has dried, paint it how you want. Draw or paint on a clown's face and stick on wool for hair.

5 Make a hat from a cone of card. Fold a narrow piece of coloured paper into a concertina and secure round the neck for a ruff. Finally add pom poms or old buttons to the hat and tummy.

FUZZY FRIENDS

CHECK OUT YOUR LOCAL ART AND CRAFT SHOP - PIPE CLEANERS AND POM POMS ARE AVAILABLE IN LOTS OF DIFFERENT COLOURS AND SIZES. TAKE A LOOK AT THE IDEAS BELOW AND THEN MAKE UP A FEW ART ATTACKS OF YOUR OWN..

COMBINE PIPE CLEANERS WITH FLUFFY POM POMS TO MAKE LOTS OF CRAZY CREATURES!

PIG

Stick a small, pink pom pom on to a larger pink pom pom. Twist four pipe cleaners round a pencil and stick them on the body to make legs. Cut a pipe cleaner in half for a tail. Cut the other half in half again, make two loops and stick on for ears. Twist another bit of a pipe cleaner to make a snout. Stick on googly eyes and two tiny black beads for nostrils.

SHEEP

Use the same method to create this cute sheep! This time add a small black pom pom to a white pom pom body, sticking a twisted pipe cleaner neck in between. Stick a further small, white pom pom on top of the head.

CAT

Stick several small pom poms together to make a long thin body for a cat. Use stripy pipe cleaners for legs and a tail. Cut out a nose from black card or foam and stick to the face. Add googly eyes and black looped ears.

FROG

For a frog, stick a large and a medium pom pom together with a pipe cleaner sandwiched in between for arms. Bend a second pipe cleaner into legs and stick on. Attach two tiny pom poms with googly eyes on the head and a small pipe cleaner mouth.

GET AHEAD

Pipe cleaners are fantastic for creating colourful hairstyles and hats! Stick the pipe cleaners to foam, polystyrene or papier maché heads.

FLOWERS AND WAND

Pipe cleaners are brilliant because you can twist them into any shape you like! Have a go at making this simple flower and wand.

EGG RACK

5 PART ATTACK

32 cm

6cm

3·5cm

1 Cut out four pieces of stiff card measuring 6cm x 32cm. On one of them draw six circles measuring 3.5cm in diameter, and cut them out.

2 Stick the four pieces together as shown. Then cut out two square pieces measuring 6cm x 6cm and tape them to each end.

3 Lay the egg rack onto a large piece of card and sketch two chickens behind it, making sure they fit the width of the rack.

PVA

4 Cut this piece out and tape it to the rack. Cover it with three layers of papier maché, building up the wings, the tails and around the head.

YOU WILL NEED:

ardboard, scissors, ruler, compass,
cky tape, PVA glue, newspaper, paints.

5 Once dry, paint as shown. Try putting your paint on in blobs of pure colour and mix gently by dabbing with your brush for a feathery effect.

COVER UP

DESIGN A COVER FOR YOUR FAVOURITE BOOK.
DON'T FORGET TO WRITE THE TITLE AND
NAME OF THE AUTHOR.

SPORTY PUPPETS

BE A SPORT AND FOLLOW THE STEPS TO MAKE THESE ENERGETIC PUPPETS!

YOU WILL NEED: PLAIN PAPER, CEREAL BOX CARD, GLUE, FELT TIP PENS, SCISSORS, PENCIL, STICKY TACK, STRING, 8 PAPER FASTENERS.

1. Over the page, you'll find your puppet pieces. Trace or photocopy the pieces onto plain paper.

2. Stick them onto cereal box card or other thin card and colour all the pieces in.

3. Carefully cut all the bits out and press holes where marked. You should make two holes in each of the limbs, four holes in the body, and one hole in the head. Push a pencil through the marked areas into a ball of sticky tack.

4. Follow pictures A and B as guides on how to fix your pieces together. You'll need four paper fasteners for each puppet.

5. Tie the small lengths of thread to each hole on the back of the puppets. Tie the pieces of string in the arms together. Do the same with the legs. Do this for both puppets.

6. Tie a length of string to the top of each puppet and hang up. Finally pull the strings and make their limbs swing!

PICTURE A

PICTURE B

NOW YOU'VE GOT THE IDEA - MAKE YOUR OWN PUPPETS WITH MOVING LIMBS! IT'S EASY!

WAX AWAY

If you draw with a wax crayon, then paint on top with watercolours, the wax will reject the paint - artists call this 'wax resist.' Try it yourself! Draw pictures or patterns using wax crayons, then mix watercolour paints with plenty of water and paint over the top.

1 Draw a picture or write a message using your coloured crayons on a piece of paper.

2 Now paint over the wax drawing using one or several colours, and leave it to dry.

CHECK OUT THESE IDEAS FOR CREATING SOME WONDERFUL WAXY PICTURES!

For fabulous fireworks, draw lines and swirls using coloured crayons, then paint over with a black or dark blue paint.

This technique is great for creating a wood effect. Draw knots and lines with crayon (yellow, brown, grey or white looks best.) then paint over with brown.

Ghosts look quite transparent! Draw them using a white crayon then paint over with a dark colour.

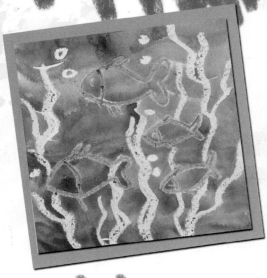

Try the wax resist for underwater scenes - draw fish, seaweed and bubbles, then overpaint with blue paint.

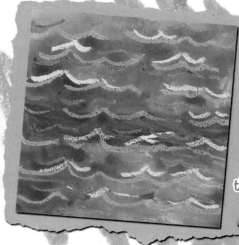

Make waves by drawing lots of little v-shapes and w-shapes with blue and white crayons, then paint over with another blue.

Flowers and leaves look great if you draw them first with coloured crayons, then paint the shapes you've drawn.

Write messages! This is a good idea for a home made birthday card - simple and quick!

41

ALIEN ATTACK!

USING A PENCIL, COPY THE ALIEN INTO THE GRID BELOW, SQUARE BY SQUARE.

COMPLETE THE PICTURE BY COLOURING IT IN WITH FELT TIP PENS AND OUTLINING IT WITH BLACK PEN.

YOU WILL NEED: Pencil, felt tip pens, black pen.

LEAF PRINTING!

Create unbe-leaf-able Art Attacks by printing with leaves!

1 Gather different shaped leaves from the ground.

2 Brush, roll or sponge paint on to the surface of the leaf and press onto white paper.

3 Carefully peel the leaf back to reveal your print. Leave it to dry.

4 Cut the prints out and stick them onto coloured card.

PRACTISE LEAF PRINTING IN THE SPACE BELOW.

POST RACK

5 PART ATTACK

1 Cut out a base about 18cm long from thick cardboard. If you don't have thick card, stick several pieces together to make it stronger.

2 Draw a piece of toast shape on a piece of thick card about 14cm high and cut it out. Make three more shapes like this.

14cm

3 Secure the toast pieces to the base equal distances apart with plenty of sticky tape.

4 Cover with three layers of torn newspaper pieces pasted on with PVA glue. Pay attention to the joins and keep it neat. Leave it to dry.

PVA

BRIGHTEN THE BREAKFAST TABLE WITH A COLOURFUL POST RACK!

YOU WILL NEED:
Cardboard box card, scissors, sticky tape, newspaper, PVA glue, paints.

5 Now decorate it. Paint the base any colour. Paint the toast pieces to look like toast using brown and white paint mixed with yellow. What about painting a fried egg on one end? Leave it to dry.

OTHER IDEAS!

WHAT ABOUT PAINTING A BIG SPLAT OF JAM ON THE OTHER END?

MAKE A MATCHING EGG CUP OUT OF CARD AND PAPIER MACHÉ AND THEN PAINT TO MATCH YOUR POST RACK.

- WHAT ABOUT GIVING IT TO MUM AS A PRESENT - IT ALSO MAKES A COOL RECIPE RACK!

SECRET CODE BREAKER

YOUR MISSION IS TO HAVE FUN MAKING THE SECRET CODE BREAKER AND THEN CRACK THE CODE.

1 Photocopy the circle below and the one on the opposite page, then stick them onto thick paper or thin card. Cut out the small window where marked.

2 Colour them both in and make a hole in the centre of each one by pushing a sharp pencil through into a ball of sticky tack.

3 Place the smaller one on top of the larger one and secure together with a paper fastener.

Make a code breaker for you and your best friend so you can tell each other secrets. No one will be able to see what you have written!

NOW HAVE A GO AT READING THE SECRET MESSAGES OVER THE PAGE....

MESSAGE ONE

6,26,26,9 - 26,2,10 - 28,26,8 - 10,18,14 -
14,16,13,10,14,8 - 13,20,14,27,1,16,6!

MESSAGE TWO

4,12 - 28,16,23,26,2,8,1,10,14 - 4,14,16,6
- 1,13 - 3,16,21,11,14,8,13 - 16,21,22 -
4,16,13,18!

47

GOLF GAME

HOW ABOUT CREATING YOUR OWN MINI CRAZY GOLF SET? INVITE YOUR MATES ROUND AND SET UP A COMPETITION.

1 Cut out several identical animal shapes from cardboard box card, making sure you cut a ball-sized hole at the bottom of each shape.

2 Cover them with three layers of papier maché and leave them to dry.

PVA

3 To make the club, cut out a shape from card as shown and fold it over one end of a stick or tightly rolled up tube of paper. Cover it with papier maché and leave it to dry.

YOU WILL NEED:
Cardboard, newspaper, PVA glue, sticky tape, card, paints and a stick (for the club)

4

Paint and decorate everything. You could stick googly eyes on your animals or just paint the eyes on.

USE STICKY TACK TO WEIGHT THE ANIMALS DOWN ON A HARD SURFACE AND GET PUTTING.

HORRIBLE GREMLIN

THIS HORRIBLE LITTLE GREMLIN IS GREAT FOR SCARING PEOPLE OUT OF YOUR BEDROOM....

7 PART ATTACK

1 Scrunch up a couple of sheets of newspaper into a ball for a head, push three dents in to make shapes for the eyes and mouth. Use sticky tape to keep it in shape.

2 Make a newspaper body and tape the head to it. You want your gremlin to be standing in a hunched, scary position.

3 Roll and fold two more sheets of newspaper to make arms and tape them to the body. Do the same for legs and tape them to a cardboard base. Make some smaller sausage shapes and stick them on to make claws.

YOU WILL NEED:

4

Tape other cardboard monster bits such as wings and horns into place to get your basic gruesome gremlin shape. Add a rolled piece of newspaper for a tail, this will help the gremlin to stand up.

IF THE WINGS DROOP WHILE THEY ARE DRYING, BALANCE SOMETHING UNDERNEATH THEM TO KEEP THEIR SHAPE.

5

Now carefully cut the base into a splat shape. If you prefer, you can do this before you secure your gremlin to it.

6

Slop plenty of diluted PVA glue all over the gremlin and base and cover with toilet roll or torn newspaper. You'll need at least three layers to make it nice and strong.

PVA

7

When dry, paint it all over in a gruesome green. Paint on streaks of other colours like brown and yellow to make it look really horrible. Let that dry before painting on eyes, a mouth, wing details and white fangs.

The Big Art Attack

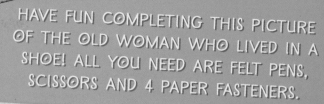

HAVE FUN COMPLETING THIS PICTURE OF THE OLD WOMAN WHO LIVED IN A SHOE! ALL YOU NEED ARE FELT PENS, SCISSORS AND 4 PAPER FASTENERS.

1 You'll find your pictures on pages 54 and 55. Photocopy the pages onto plain paper.

2 Stick them onto thin card and then cut out the main picture and the smaller pictures using the dotted lines as a guide. Colour everything in.

3 Make holes where marked on the main picture at points A, B, C and D. Similarly, make holes in the smaller pictures at points A, B, C and D.

4 Now cut small slits at sections A and B, where marked. Cut out section C.

5 Finally, using paper fasteners, fix the smaller pictures to the main picture matching the correct ones up.

53

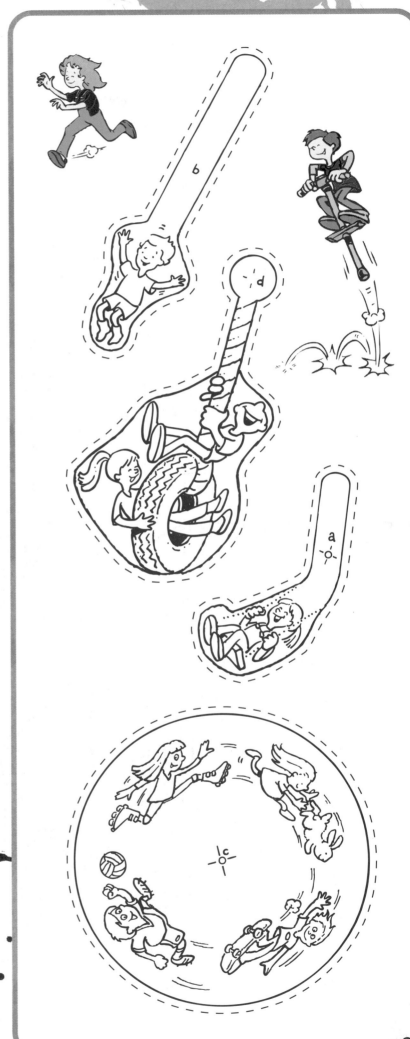

QUICK ATTACK
Beauty Box

TAKE AN OLD SHOEBOX AND TRANSFORM IT INTO A UNIQUE ART ATTACK. HOW ABOUT A BRILLIANT BEAUTY BOX OR A GAME TO PLAY WITH YOUR FRIENDS?

You will need a shoebox with a lid, tin foil, sticky tape, newspaper, PVA glue, paints and a black marker pen.

1 Cut the edges off the lid and stick to one long side of the box.

2 Cover the box and lid, inside and out with two layers of papier maché. Leave it to dry.

3 Attach a square of tin foil to the inside of the lid with sticky tape.

4 Now paint your beauty box any colour you like.

5 Finally add details with black marker pen.

PUT SOME TISSUE PAPER IN THE BOTTOM AND THEN FILL IT WITH ALL YOUR FAVOURITE STUFF!

Target Game!

You will need a shoebox with a lid, scissors, paints and a black marker pen.

1 Carefully cut a circle from the middle of the lid.

2 Paint the whole thing, including the lid one colour. Leave it to dry.

3 Paint target circles on the lid, around the circle you've cut away.

4 Finally paint or write numbers in the circles so you know how many points you score.

NOW THROW SCRUNCHED UP PIECES OF PAPER AT THE BOX AND SEE HOW MANY POINTS YOU CAN SCORE!

FLIPPED OUT

WHAT TO DO:

1 Photocopy pages 58 and 59 onto plain paper.

2 Stick the pages on to thick paper and colour all the characters in with felt tip pens or coloured pencils.

3 Cut the eight characters out and then cut along all of the red lines up to the dotted lines.

4 Place the characters on top of each other, aligning the head, body and leg sections.

5 Glue or staple along the spine to make a book.

6 Finally, flip out! Open the book to mix 'n' match the heads, bodies and legs!

HOW ABOUT CREATING YOUR OWN FUNNY FLIP BOOK? CREATE THE BOOKLET IN THE SAME WAY, THEN DRAW YOUR OWN COLLECTION OF CREATURES!

ART ATTACK

HOW TO DR

DRAWING PIN PEOPLE IS EASY AND IT'S A FANTASTIC WAY TO LEARN HOW TO DRAW THE BODY IN VARIOUS POSITIONS. CHECK OUT THE BASIC SHAPE, THEN TRY A FEW OF YOUR OWN.

Head   Spine   Shoulders   Hips   Upper arms/thighs   Forearm/lower leg   Hands/feet

TRY IT YOURSELF

NOW YOU HAVE SEEN HOW IT'S DONE, COMPLETE THE 'PINBOARD' BELOW

MAKE A SNAKE

WHAT A CARD!

Cut out circles of coloured card - as many as you like. Punch holes in the sides of each one and secure together with paper fasteners. Glue on a forked tongue and some googly eyes! Now make him wiggle!

SEW COOL!

Cut out circles of card. Cut out a head and tail shape. Punch holes in either side of each circle and then fasten together with a long length of string or ribbon, lacing it through the holes. It's a bit like doing up your shoe laces! Add stickers to decorate.

TOP STUFF!

Recycle bottle tops into a foil snake! Collect loads of clean milk bottle tops. Fold the edges under, then thread on to a strong sewing thread using a darning needle. For the head and tail use crumpled balls of kitchen foil.

63

THIS TRACE IT IS DEAD FUN! SIMPLY TRACE ALL THE PICTURES FROM BELOW ON TO THE RIGHT-HAND PICTURE TO CREATE A GRUESOME GRAVEYARD SCENE.

M...M...MAKE A MOSAIC

You will need:

Coloured paper, thick card, glue, scissors, googly eyes.

1 Trace the penguin, and stick it onto thick card.

2 Cut out or rip up lots of tiny, coloured squares of paper. You'll need black, red, blue and yellow.

3 Using the glue, stick the squares on the penguin following this picture as a guide.

4 Finally stick on two googly eyes.

IF YOU DON'T HAVE COLOURED PAPER, USE AN OLD COMIC OR MAGAZINE.

66

CLAY FRAME

Say it with clay! Make a fabulous frame from clay and give it away as a picture perfect gift

1 Roll your clay into a large 3mm thick rectangle – it can be any size. Using a plastic knife, cut a rectangle out from the centre, leaving a 3cm border all the way round. Put it aside to harden.

2 To decorate the frame. You can make anything you want. This one has tiny creatures and leaves.

3 Once you have made some things, push them gently onto the hardening frame and then leave it all to harden (depending on the clay instructions.)

4 When the frame is hard, paint it and then leave it to dry.

5 Now paint the leaves green adding darker green stripes to illustrate the veins.

6 Paint all the bugs and flowers.

7 Leave it to dry, then stick a picture to the back.

8 Give it to someone special or hang it up in your room!

YOU WILL NEED:
Self-hardening clay, plastic knife, paint.

HOT TIP!
To hang it up, make a hole in the back and stick a piece of looped string in it. As the clay hardens the string will become a secure hook.

ARTY ACTIVITIES

CHECK OUT THESE LITTLE BRAINTEASERS WHILE YOU'RE WAITING FOR THAT PAINT TO DRY.

WORD FIT

Place these 8 arty words in the grid below – they only fit in one place.

ART   GLUE
PAINT   PENCIL
BRUSH   PAPER
SCISSORS   NEWSPAPER

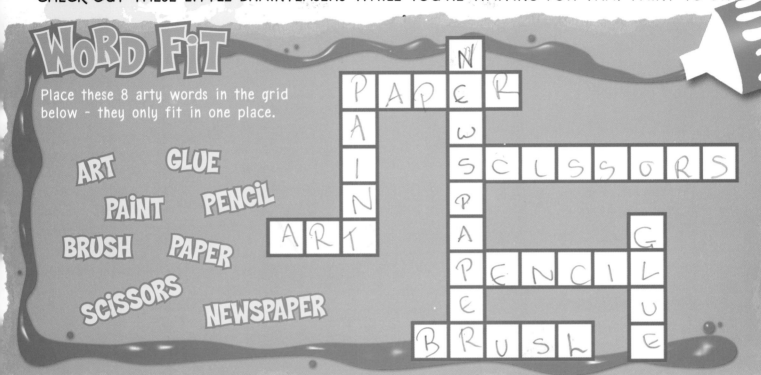

BRUSH UP

How many paintbrushes can you count below?

SPLAT ATTACK

What colour should the final splat be below?

69

SHELF BUG

EVEN IF YOU'RE NOT KEEN ON CREEPY CRAWLIES, YOU'LL LIKE THESE GIANT BUGS.

5 PART ATTACK

1

To make a body, roll two sheets of newspaper around a toilet roll tube and bind it with sticky tape. Add extra padding with crumpled newspaper to help form the shape, which should be thinner at the top and flat at the bottom.

2

Crumple a sheet of newspaper into a ball, secure it with sticky tape and stick to the narrow end of the body.

YOU WILL NEED:

For each bug: 7 pipe cleaners, 7 plastic straws, newspaper, sticky tape, 2 beads, PVA glue, paints, 1 cardboard tube, tissue paper or kitchen roll, pair of googly eyes.

3

Tape two pipe cleaners to the underside of the body and slip straws over them. Where the pipe cleaner pokes out, bend it back to form a foot.

4

Make holes in the sides of the body and stick a pipe cleaner into each one. Trim straws to the required length and slip them over the pipe cleaners. Do the same for the antennae.

5

Cover everything with three layers of papier maché and leave it to dry. Then paint your bug and stick on googly eyes. Stick beads to the antennae.

GO AS WILD AS YOU LIKE- CREATE LOTS OF DIFFERENT COLOURED BUGS.

TaKe NoTiC

DO YOU WANT TO CREATE A STRIKING FUNKY POSTER OR INNOVATIVE INVITATION? WELL YOU NEED TO CHECK OUT THIS IDEA - IT'S GREAT FUN AND DEAD EASY.

1 Cut a plain piece of card to the size you want - large for a poster or small for an invitation.

2 Think about what you want to say on your poster or invitation and then cut out lots of different letters from a magazine - different shapes and styles!

3 Stick these letters on a plain white piece of paper to spell out your message.

4 Tear the edges of the paper and curl them up a bit. Rub your fingertip on a pencil tip and then rub the paper to make it look grubby.

5 To make the background, dip the sides of a rubber into two different brick-coloured paints and stamp across the card to create a brick wall. Leave a space in between the prints. For a large poster use a sponge instead of a rubber.

6 When the background is dry, put the message piece onto the background and pin it in place using four drawing pins.

THIS IS A GREAT POSTER TO BRIGHTEN UP THE CLASSROOM OR YOUR BEDROOM. SIMPLY MAKE A NEW MESSAGE WHEN YOU WANT TO CHANGE WHAT IT SAYS

MAKING FACES

WHAT A JOKE

THIS ART ATTACK JOKE BOOK IS FUN TO MAKE AND IS A GREAT WAY TO GIVE YOUR FRIENDS A LAUGH,

YOU WILL NEED:

Plain paper,
scissors,
glue,
felt tips pens,
stapler.

 1 Over the page you'll find all the pages, including the cover, of your joke book. Photocopy these pages and stick them onto plain paper.

 2 Colour in all the pictures and then cut the two pages out around the dotted lines.

 3 Stick both pages back to back using paper glue. When it's dry, cut it into three sections so that you have separate double pages such as 1 and 10 with the cover and back cover on the reverse, and so on.

 4 Now put the pages together, using the drawing as a guide. Staple the pages in the middle to form a little book.

glue

fold + staple

DREAM ON

WHAT DO YOU DREAM ABOUT? LET EVERYONE KNOW WITH THIS COOL DREAM CLOUD. YOU CAN CHANGE THE PICTURE EACH TIME YOUR DREAMS COME TRUE

1 Draw a 'think bubble' on a piece of cardboard box card. Then draw the inside of the cloud shape in the middle. Cut it out - including the centre.

2 From card scraps, cut out different sized circles ranging from large ones to really small ones.

3 Cover the cloud and circles with three layers of papier maché. Leave them to dry.

4 Paint the cloud and circles white. When they are dry, dab the edges with pale blue using a fairly dry brush. Finally go around the edges with a black marker pen. Now stick the circles together to form a chain, as shown in the main picture.

4 PART ATTACK

HOT TIPS

YOU CAN MAKE ANY SHAPED DREAM OR SPEECH BUBBLE YOU LIKE. ROUNDED, SPIKEY, LARGE OR SMALL.

STICK IT ABOVE YOUR BED SO EVERYONE CAN SEE WHAT YOU'RE DREAMING ABOUT - ESPECIALLY GOOD AROUND YOUR BIRTHDAY

EYE MASKS

BUZZY BEE

1

Trace the eye template from the opposite page and draw around it on to a piece of yellow card.

2

Glue strips of black paper across the shape you have drawn, then cut it out around the outline.

3

Trace the wing template, cut two from tracing paper and draw veins in pencil. Stick them in place.

4

For antennae, glue pom poms on the ends of two short pipe cleaners and glue the other ends in place on the mask.

5

Finally, make a small hole either side of the eye piece and thread string or elastic though.

BEAUTIFUL BUTTERFLY

THE BUTTERFLY EYE MASK IS MADE IN A SIMILAR WAY TO THE BEE, EXCEPT THE WINGS ARE CUT FROM CARD.

TRY TO FIND METALLIC CARD FOR A SHIMMERING EFFECT. CUT SHAPES FROM SCRAPS OF COLOURED PAPER OR CARD TO DECORATE THE WINGS.

CHOOSE YOUR OWN COLOUR COMBINATIONS.

YOU WILL NEED:

Yellow card, black paper, tracing paper, pencil, pom poms, pipe cleaners, glue, card, string or elastic.

USE THE EYE MASK TEMPLATE TO CREATE ALL SORTS OF DIFFERENT MASKS.

FAIRY TALE

5 PART ATTACK

RECYCLE LOTS OF BITS'N'BOBS INTO A FUNKY FAIRY LIKE THIS ONE. AND HERE'S HOW...

YOU WILL NEED:

2 paper cups, newspaper, straw, PVA glue, 2 buttons, needle and thread, paint, sequins, shiny card, tinsel, sticky tack, googly eyes, wool.

1

Make the body from two paper cups placed one inside the other. Attach a head made from a scrunched up ball of newspaper. Stick a length of straw into the head and through the bottom of the cups to make a neck.

2 Make thin sausages of newspaper for legs. Add little scrunched up bits to make knobbly knees and larger crumpled bits to make the feet. Cover the head, body and legs with three layers of papier mâché and leave them to dry.

3 To make the arms, cut the tops off two drinking straws. Thread some cotton through a button, through the top of one of the straws, through the cup and out the other side. Thread it through the second straw and second button. Tie tightly.

Paint the fairy and add sequins to the dress. Stick on some wool hair and googly eyes. Paint the legs and secure in the cup with a large ball of sticky tack.

4

5 Add a mouth and nose, and stick on some fairy wings made from shiny card. Make a crown from glittery paper and glue tinsel round her neck.

DESIGN A STRIP

EVER FANCIED MANAGING YOUR OWN TEAM OR ARE YOU JUST A MASSIVE FOOTIE FAN? EITHER WAY YOU CAN HAVE FUN DESIGNING YOUR OWN STRIP!

1 Photocopy the black and white picture several times so you can practise drawing your unique strip.

2 Alternatively you can trace the picture onto plain paper.

3 Use felt tip pens or coloured pencils to colour in the footballer. Use black felt pen to outline any stripes or patterns.

4 Finally, design a team badge and colour the fans in.

5 PART ATTACK

MAKE SOME UNIQUE GIFT BOXES FOR YOUR FRIENDS AND FAMILY. THEY MAKE GREAT PENCIL CASES TOO!

1 Cut out an oval shape like this one. Cut out another one about 4mm larger all the way round. These form the base and the lid of your gift box.

2 Cut a piece of bendy card about 4cm wide and long enough to go around the base. Secure this to the base with sticky tape, following the picture as a guide.

3 Do the same to the lid but make the card only 2cm wide. Check that the lid fits easily on to the base. Separate the lid and base.

4cm

2cm

RRECT

get well soon

Happy Bathday

PVA

4 Cover both halves with two layers of torn newspaper pasted on with diluted PVA glue, keeping it neat. Leave them to dry.

5 Now decorate! Paint the inside black card and the outside any colour you like. Label them how you wish.

JUMBO SNACK

CHECK OUT THIS TASTY MAKE.

YOU WILL NEED:

Cardboard box card, card, sticky tape, newspaper, PVA glue, paint, green tissue paper.

5 PART ATTACK

1 Cut all the pieces from card. You'll need two circles for the bun, two for the burgers, several smaller round pieces for the tomatoes, a few rounded, triangular shapes for the gherkins, two square pieces for the cheese and some long pieces for the chips.

2 Pad out the burger and chip pieces with newspaper. Do the same with all the other pieces. Cover them all with two layers of papier maché and leave them to dry.

3 Make the bun by padding out the card with scrunched up newspaper. Make the top bun more rounded and fatter and the bottom piece more flat. Cover with two layers of papier maché and leave them to dry.

4 Make the chip box by cutting out this shape from card. Make the sides about 9cm long and the middle 8cm wide. Fold it as shown and stick it together. Cover with two layers of papier maché and leave it to dry.

5 Paint all the pieces and leave them to dry. Put your burger together, gluing the pieces in as you go. Add some green tissue for lettuce. Finally put the chips into the box.

8cm

9cm

CHECK OUT THESE TIPS FOR DRAWING REFLECTIONS, IT'S SIMPLE ONCE YOU KNOW HOW!

Create a picture such as this desert island from simple shapes.

Trace the image with a soft pencil, flip the tracing paper over and then rub the back with the pencil to create the reflection.

AW.... REFLECTIONS

Do the same with this picture of a swan...

Make reflections blurry or smudged-looking with your finger...

When you're happy with your final image, colour it to complete.

TRY IT YOURSELF

COMPLETE THIS GIRL'S REFLECTION BY ADDING FACIAL FEATURES AND DETAILS ON HER CLOTHES.

FrEaKy FriEnds

CREATE THESE COOL, CREEPY CREATURES! ALL YOU NEED IS WOOL, PIPE CLEANERS, CARD, SCISSORS AND GOOGLY EYES. (YOU CAN MAKE EYES FROM CARD IF YOU PREFER.)

WHAT TO DO:

1 Cut two circles from card and then cut a hole in the middle of both circles.

2 Place the two circles on top of each other and wrap wool around them until it is quite thick. Tie it in place.

3 Using scissors, cut the wool around the outside edge of the card, in between the two circles, and tie in place with string.

4 Remove the card and fluff out the wool to form a pom pom shape.

5 Finally stick on some googly eyes and a paper mouth and hang it up!

MAKE LOTS OF DANGLY CREATURES AND THEN HANG THEM AROUND THE HOUSE - THEY'LL LOOK BRILLIANT AT A THEMED PARTY.

BEARING GIFTS

5 PART ATTACK

A little book of sentiments FOR A SPECIAL *friend*

Mr. P. Bear
Igloo nº 3
North pole

Mr. P. Bear
Igloo nº
N-

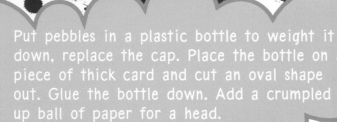

Put pebbles in a plastic bottle to weight it down, replace the cap. Place the bottle on a piece of thick card and cut an oval shape out. Glue the bottle down. Add a crumpled up ball of paper for a head.

94

Cardboard, plastic bottle, pebbles, newspaper, scissors, sticky tape, PVA glue, paints.

2 Pad out the bottle, more thickly at the base, with newspaper. Roll them into sausage shapes and tape in position.

3 Cut a rectangle of card the same width as the height of the bottle (not including the head). Snip down from the top to about halfway at 2cm intervals. Wrap it around the newspaper, overlapping the snipped pieces and tape it down.

4 Make arms with rolled up card, tape in place with the hands together. Cut out ear shapes and stick to the head, tape feet shapes to the bottom.

5 Pad out the feet with balls of crumpled paper and then cover the whole thing with three layers of torn paper pasted on with diluted PVA glue. When it's dry, paint it.

PVA

TRACE IT

Bring this funny farmyard to life by tracing the pictures below onto the right-hand page. The small pictures go in the background and the larger pictures go in the foreground.

DOUGH ROBOTS

SALT DOUGH RECIPE

2 cups flour
1 cup salt
1 cup water
2 tablespoons vegetable oil

YOU WILL NEED:

Mixing bowl,
Large spoon,
Food colouring,
4-6 small plastic bags,
Aluminium foil,
Drinking straws,
Drawing pins, Safety pins
Bulldog clip, Sequins
Nails, Screws, Beads

WARNING:
ADULT SUPERVISION IS RECOMMENDED

1. Mix together the flour and salt.

2. Add the water and oil. Stir with the spoon and then use your hands to mix it thoroughly.

3. Separate the dough into several blobs and place each blob in a seperate plastic bag, add a few drops of food colouring to each blob to make a different colour. Knead the blobs in the bags to mix the colour in.

4. Lay down a sheet of aluminium foil and begin your robot by rolling out one of the blobs to make a body. Add a head, arms and legs, using different coloured blobs.

5. Use all your bits 'n' bobs to give your robot character. Use all sorts of colourful junk to decorate them; just check out the pictures to get some ideas!

6. Finally let the dough dry overnight before removing from the foil.

CRAZY CAMEL

1 To make the body, cut a piece of cardboard about 25cm x 30cm and roll it into a cylinder. Tape the edges together.

2 Stand the cylinder upright on a scrap of card, squash it slightly, then draw around the end. Cut out two of these oval shapes. Tape to either end.

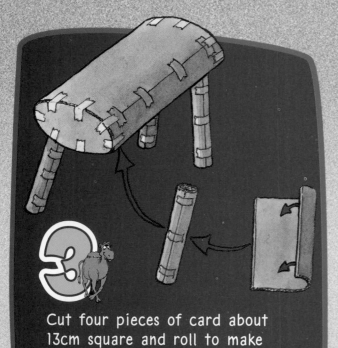

3 Cut four pieces of card about 13cm square and roll to make legs. Tape in place to the body.

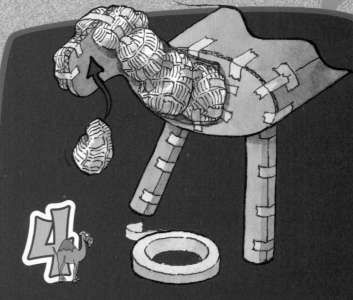

4 Cut a head shape from card and build it up with scrunched paper secured with sticky tape. Attach it to the body.

HERE'S AN IDEA- WHY DON'T YOU CREATE A COMICAL CAMEL PENCIL POT? IT WON'T GIVE YOU THE HUMP.

YOU WILL NEED:

Bendy card, card, sticky tape, newspaper, kitchen roll, 2 paper cups, PVA glue, straw, paints, string or ribbon.

5 For humps, tape on two paper cups with the bases cut off. Wrap the cups with several layers of kitchen roll to create a more rounded shape.

6 Attach a cut down straw with sticky tape to make a tail. Stick a bobble of paper on the end.

7 Cover the camel with about three layers of torn newspaper pasted on with diluted PVA glue, paying attention to all the joins. Leave it to dry.

8 Paint the camel white all over and leave it to dry. Then paint it a yellowy brown colour. When that is dry, add details on the face. Finally attach a piece of string or ribbon for reins.

Wooden Spoon Puppets

THE SHAPE OF A WOODEN SPOON IS PERFECT FOR MAKING PUPPETS. USE YOUR IMAGINATION TO CREATE FAIRY TALE CHARACTERS, MONSTERS, POP STARS, ANYTHING YOU CAN THINK OF! START WITH THIS PRINCE AND PRINCESS...

1 Paint or draw a face on your wooden spoon.

2 Add hair – You can plait yellow wool and stick it on with glue for the princess.

3 Wrap a pipecleaner around the spoon and secure in place with tape or glue. Bend the ends around to form hands.

4 Fold a piece of fabric around the spoon – make small holes in the sides and pull the pipecleaners through. Glue the fabric in place.

5 Add a fake fur trim around the neck and stick on any jewels or sequins.

YOU WILL NEED:

Wooden spoons, paint, pieces of fabric, pipe cleaners, fake fur, felt, plastic jewels, glue, gold card, ribbon.

6 Finish off with a crown cut from gold card. Stick a jewel on the front and secure to the head.

7 For the prince's hair – cut short lengths of brown wool and glue them to his head.

8 Make a cloak from a square of felt. Give the cloak a fake fur trim with white fabric or cotton wool. Make clasps and ties from jewels and ribbon.

9 Smarten up the royal gown with some strips of ribbon glued down the front.

TOP TIP!

If you want to be clever – make a double-sided spoon. Paint a face on both sides and decorate the front and back slightly differently. Stick the hair on just the sides. Now flip your spoon to make a quick character change!

FOOTIE FUN

CHECK OUT THIS MINI TABLE TOP FOOTBALL GAME.

YOU WILL NEED:

Card, pencil, tracing paper, scissors, felt tips, small cardboard box, sticky tape, marble, straws.

WHAT TO DO:

1. Using the template, trace two goalies onto card and cut them both out. Draw a number 1 on their tops.

2. Use the other template of a football player to trace your teams onto card. You could have a 5-a-side team or you could have more players – it's up to you!

3. Cut out all your players and write numbers on their kit. Split them into teams and colour their kit in your chosen colours. Change the colour of their hair so that they look different.

4. Make little snips in each of their feet. Cut out small rectangles of card and slot them into these slits so your footballers stand up.

5. Make two goals by cutting a small cardboard box in half and painting it white. When it has dried, use black marker pen to draw lines on it.

HOW TO PLAY:

⚽ YOU AND A FRIEND PLACE YOUR TWO TEAMS IN POSITION WITH THE GOALS AND GOALIES ON A TABLE.

⚽ GET A MARBLE AND PLACE IT IN THE MIDDLE.

⚽ USE STRAWS TO BLOW THE MARBLE THROUGH THE OTHER TEAMS LEGS AND SCORE A GOAL.

⚽ WHOEVER SCORES THE MOST GOALS AFTER 5 MINUTES IS THE WINNER. IF IT'S A DRAW, GO TO PENALTIES!

107

PAINT PALETTE

1 Draw a palette shape onto cardboard box card. Cut it out and cut a hole in it. This is the lid. Place it onto another piece of card and draw around it. Cut it out about 2mm inside this line, to make a smaller palette shape for the base.

2 Cut a strip of paint card box wide and long enough to go around the lid edge. Tape it in place. Cut a strip 2cm wide and do the same to make the base. Check that the lid fits onto the base.